Book one
of the
Divine Dark Feminine series

Exploring the path of the
ancient goddess
in a modern world

Sedna
Loving the Unloved

BY

Fi Woods

'For my sister, Sedna, with love and for anyone who feels unloved or unwanted'

All rights reserved, no part of this publication may be either reproduced or transmitted by any means whatsoever without the prior permission of the publisher.

VENEFICIA PUBLICATIONS UK

Editing Veneficia Publications & Fi Woods
Typesetting © Veneficia Publications
Text © Fi Woods
October 2020
veneficiapublications.com
veneficiapublications@gmail.com

Cover image - public domain

CONTENTS

1	Introduction
2	Mother of the Sea
10	An Invisible but not Unforgotten God
17	Finding the Missing Pieces Within my Spiritual Twin
22	Transformation
27	Natural Majic
36	Being Human
39	Simple

I saw also that there was an ocean of darkness and death, but an infinite ocean of light and love, which flowed over the ocean of darkness.

George Fox

INTRODUCTION

The feminine goddess, the dark and wanton harlots and the loving mother - all of which have a place not only in the world but within each and every one of us: our shadow side, our lost moments, regrets, resentments and heartaches.

The dark and divine feminine aspects exist in all of us and have always done so. This book explores several of those darker emotions, whether thrust upon us or of our own doing heartbreak affects us in some way. It is not wrong to feel anger, jealousy, nor is it wrong to feel lust and desire. What makes us good or evil largely depends on our actions and reactions when faced with these darker, less socially acceptable emotions and aspects of self

This book looks at Sedna; a feminine deity who despite the harsh words, cruelty and vicious abuse she experienced from those who should love her and whom she should be able to trust, became the mother of all marine life. A goddess whose darker emotions created some of the most beautiful creatures and plants the world has ever seen along with some of the most terrible.

MOTHER OF THE SEA

Those of you reading this book probably already have some knowledge of gods and goddesses, and those of them who are considered the "dark" entities.

I'd like to introduce you to a dark feminine deity with whom you may be somewhat less familiar: Sedna, Inuit goddess of the sea and marine animals, and ruler of the Inuit underworld Adlivun.

She is described as a "vengeful" goddess and one of her alternate names, *Arnapkapfaaluk*, translates as "Big Bad Woman." She is also known as Arnakuagsak, Arnaqquassaaq, Nuliajuk, Takannaaluk, or Sassuma Arnaa meaning Mother of the Deep or Mother of the Sea.

There are at least five legends associated with Sedna, all of which feature the mutilation of her hand/s, and it doesn't matter which of Sedna's stories you choose to believe because all of the legends around her are nothing short of tragic, and anyone who isn't touched by at least one of them must be made of stone.

It's interesting and very darkly ironic that in one version Sedna is the only child of Anguta, a psychopomp whose name means "man with something to cut." Did he cut her fingers off because of his name or was he named because he cut her fingers off? Sedna was a giant and her huge appetite made her attack her parents. Anguta took her out to sea and threw her out of his kayak; as she desperately clutched the edge of the boat, her own father cut her fingers off to ensure her death by drowning. Her fingers became the seals, walruses, and whales that were hunted by the Inuit. It strikes me as horrendously *dark* that after killing Sedna, her father delivered the dead to her – she had to see him constantly, is that not seriously rubbing salt into the wounds?

Or that she married a dog because she did not like the men her father found for her; her father reacts as in the previous legend.

In another version Sedna is so beautiful that all the hunters in her village attempt to woo her, but she turns them all down. When a stranger appears, Sedna's father agrees that he can have her in exchange for fish. Sedna's given a sleeping potion by her dad and handed over to the stranger, who takes her to a nest on the cliffs where he reverts to his true form: a great bird-spirit. When Sedna wakes up, finding birds all around her, her father tries to rescue her, but the bird-spirit causes a great storm and her father throws her into the sea.

Again, she clings desperately to her father's kayak, but her hands freeze, and her fingers fall off.

Alternatively, she is kidnapped by a bird and imprisoned on an ice-island. Her father rescues her while her kidnapper is away, but he is furious when he finds her gone and calls a sea spirit to help him. The spirit finds the kayak and throws huge waves at it to kill Sedna and her father. Her father throws Sedna overboard, hoping to appease the spirit; Sedna hangs on desperately, but her father cuts off her fingers and bashes her on the head for good measure.

Of all Sedna's legends, the one which touches me the most and hurts me the most is the tale of her as an orphan, unwanted by *everybody* in her village; those villagers subsequently mutilating and killing her. Again, her death involved her fingers being cut off followed by drowning.

As well as the mutilation, there are other themes which are present in all of Sedna's legends: punishment, abandonment, imprisonment, cruelty, brutality, loss, grief, fear, despair, desperation. She was unloved, unwanted, and constantly subjected to rejection: she was always thrown away, discarded.

These are all experiences and feelings which have characterised and shaped my own life; from as far back as I can remember to the present. That's roughly 47 years now, and I strongly suspect that these feelings will be with me all the way to the clearing at the end of the path (many thanks to Stephen King for that particular phrase, which resonates with me).

Do you have any idea how it feels to be completely unwanted, of no worth or value to anyone? I do, and it's a feeling that's almost impossible to adequately convey in words. It's one of those "If you haven't been there you can't really understand it" situations. The thing is that when you show such a total lack of humanity towards a person, it touches that person for ever. It burns them with scars that seldom heal.

My first 13 years or so, from about 3 to 16 were nothing but cruelty, brutality, and punishment at the hands of an adoptive parent. I wasn't loved, I wasn't wanted: my family just wanted rid of me. I may not have been physically mutilated, but I was certainly emotionally and psychologically mutilated. I wasn't dealt physical abuse or physically killed, the abuse hurled at me was verbal but led to the psychological destruction of the child I was and the adult I could have become.

I, like Sedna in two of her other legends, refused matches that were made for me by my dominant parent; I would not, could not, become involved with the men or the careers that were considered suitable for me. (What it *really* meant is that they were suitable for the *family's perceived social standing*; none of it was about *me* or *my* happiness).

I was an outcast within my family; and then cast out.

This long-term inescapable experience not only caused fear, despair and desperation, but it also taught me to never expect anything else.

Be it self-fulfilling prophecy or not, it is nonetheless the case that these feelings have travelled with me into the vast majority of my relationships, my social interactions, and pretty much every other area of my life.

Wherever I have been, whatever I have done, I have remained caught in their web.

I have been trapped by them, imprisoned by them and, having spent roughly half of my life so far in mental units following repeated suicide attempts, I have also in a very real sense lost my life to them. Sedna and I are both dead; it's just that I am currently only dead on the inside.

To many people, suicide and depression are *selfish* and nothing more than *self-pity*. 'Why don't you think of others?' I am asked . 'How are those you leave behind going to feel?'

Is it not *selfish* that others expect me to continue being so unhappy in a life that they would not want, nor have to, live? Why do I have to stay alive for *them*? What about *me*? Why don't *I* matter? Why don't *my* feelings count?

As for self-pity; I don't, and never have, felt that within me. It's always simply being unable to deal with all of the hurt, pain, sorrow, grief, loss, and anguish within me.

I have been thrown away, discarded, like Sedna. I have no pity or compassion for myself, but for her I weep.

I feel *so* much compassion, *so* much love for Sedna; I wish it were possible to hold her in my arms and tell her how much she means to me, to let her know that she is not alone. If only I could say to her 'You are no longer alone, unloved, and unwanted. I am with you, always, and *you are very much loved and wanted.*'

Sedna suffered horrendously, in all of her legends; my heart and my soul *hurt* for her, for all that she went through. I *feel* her pain and I *ache* at my inability to give her comfort; I have no way of righting the wrongs that were done to her, however much I may wish to do so.

But I tell her these things in the hope that she can hear me; if she can hear me, perhaps I am giving her some comfort.

And I continue to wish, and I continue to hope.

My "legacy" after my death is most likely to be memories of me as someone that it was difficult, if not impossible, to be friends with. Someone who could not successfully have an intimate relationship. Someone who was deeply troubled and constantly struggled with life. Happily, Sedna's death has (and there's no way of wording this without it sounding daft) been more positive than her life. She *has* not been forgotten and her name will continue to be remembered far beyond my death and me talking about her. Other people know about her and have brought her into modern history and culture: for example, in 1980, Sedna featured on a Canadian postage stamp, in 2003, a minor planet was discovered and named 90377 Sedna, and *Apricot Blush*'s 2018 album *Where Blew a Flower, May a Flower No More* tells Sedna's story through songs.

Sedna lives, and always will.

She is not forgotten, and never will be.

Thrown away, no love, no care
Abandoned, alone, but oh so aware
What did I do? What was so wrong?
Heartlessly killed, no chance to live long
My blood stains the water, consigned to the deep
The oceans merge with the tears that I weep

Yet from all my sorrow new life hails
The seals, walruses, and the whales
All who hurt me catch their feed
While I lie here wearing the drifting seaweed
It's said I am nasty, vengeful, and mean
But it's just for some kindness that I keen
Helpless against others, nobody wanted me
I am Sedna, Mother of the Sea
©Fi Woods

AN INVISIBLE BUT NOT UNFORGOTTEN GOD

I was not only brought up Catholic, but my dominant parent very openly talked about her belief that the God who listened to and loved *her* was not the same God who listened to and loved the Jews, the Muslims, the Niggers (yes, that's the word she used), the gays ...

This completely baffled me, even as a child I just could not comprehend it: exactly how many of these invisible men who could walk on water and turn it into wine was I meant to believe in?

At that young age I could, at a real stretch, have *possibly* believed in *one* such being; but I could not and would not, believe that every culture, every race and possibly every person had their own divine, loving, invisible being, who answered all their prayers and forgave them all the wrongs that they committed against others.

If such a being did, in fact exist, he would surely love all people equally; would he not?

Unable to reconcile any of what I was taught as a child, I rejected it all and grew up with no faith or belief except for this: whatever people called their religion/faith/belief it served two purposes and neither of them were good.

Firstly, each person interpreted it to suit themselves and used it as a prop/crutch to get them through their lives and safely into "heaven," secondly, it was used as a reason for humanity to commit atrocities against humanity, causing endless wars and killing. But it was *all ok*, because it was all *done in the name* of whatever religion/faith/belief.

I *hated* religion and became very strongly opposed to it. Kind of militantly atheistic I guess; thinking back on it.

Formal education at this time focused solely on the Christian God. Other faiths, beliefs, gods, or goddesses were completely omitted. It's possible that I would have been taught about all these others if I had chosen Religious Education as an option, but as an unbeliever with no faith I didn't do so, and I'm not sure that that would have been the case back then anyway.

It wasn't until many years later, around 2010, that I had a conversation with a friend in which she talked to me about paganism, Wicca, other belief systems and other deities.

This friend, who coincidentally is herself surely an example of the dark feminine, and I have known each other for far longer than either of us cares to remember; yet she had never mentioned any of this to me before.

She had not talked to me about her beliefs or her faith, and I wondered why that was. Asking her provided no real answer, and I wonder if it was something that she held to herself until I *needed* to hear about it, until it was the *right* time for *me*.

I had left this place where I grew up in 2002: an attempt to outrun all my hurt, to outrun myself, to find a new me, to find a *life*. These were the *hidden* reasons though; reasons that I didn't realise or recognise at the time.

What I *did* know at the time was that I had to go elsewhere in order to pursue my ambition, my vocation. I had known which career path I wanted to follow since I was a young teenager, but after leaving school and trying to enter that profession I was brutally told by the powers that be that my dream would not be achievable in my home town: 'We would *never* employ someone like *you*.'

There were no acceptable reasons for this refusal; the plain fact was that the council who would be my employers were very conservative, and I blatantly was not. I tried to argue my case, but their stance was firm and unchanging.

I met a man and moving away then happened very quickly; too quickly, with the wonders of hindsight.

I packed, handed in my

council house, took my son, and moved in with this man. (Needless to say, really, that relationship didn't work out and lasted no time at all.)

My son's father begged me not to leave and pleaded in tears for me not to take his son away, but my mind was set and off I went. I recently asked his forgiveness for taking his son away, for not listening to him, for not discussing it with him, and he gave it readily. I haven't yet forgiven myself for it, and I have no idea when I will or whether I will ever be able to do so.

My new council took me on immediately and I sailed through training, finishing with two offers of employment. I took both.

I was working within my chosen field, I had achieved my ambition and loved my work. I was happy and fulfilled; and I felt *normal*; it seemed that I had finally moved beyond my parent's abuse and become a *real* person.

It all crashed after about 30 months, when someone died. I felt responsible for that death and had a breakdown.

Unsurprisingly, my way of dealing with it, after I came out of the loony bin, was to uproot my son and move yet again.

I returned to work (yep, another council who employed me

straight away), but although I still loved my work I was not the same.

The death still weighed heavily on me, I constantly had nightmares about it (and still do). My ability to cope, my façade of normality was becoming hard to maintain. Several more breakdowns occurred and after several hospitalisations, I dealt with the situation by moving.

Quelle surprise.

I had absolutely no trouble gaining employment; again, being offered, and taking, two jobs.

The death stayed with me, affecting my work. I became scared that the same thing would happen, and that fear rendered me less effective as a worker.

My ability to cope vanished, my parent's impact returned with a vengeance and I fell apart; completely traumatised.

Breakdown followed breakdown, hospitalisation followed hospitalisation.

I made the decision to resign, to acknowledge that I was no longer capable of fulfilling the demands of my job effectively. My line manager begged me not to leave, and it hurt me a *lot* to do so, but my honour and integrity knew that it was the *right* thing to do.

I had fully reverted to being what my parent said I was; not only *being* but also *believing*. I was back to being useless, worthless, unlovable...

I had run and run but the escape was only ever temporary; an illusion.

For the final decade or so my suicide attempts were increasing in frequency (but obviously not increasing in effectiveness) and the sea was calling me back with an ever-louder voice.

Having reached the point where I so badly missed the sea that I was waking each morning *already* in tears, I finally decided to come Home. To the Island? Yes, unquestionably so; but more importantly, to the sea.

That move took place *exactly* 9 years ago as I write this; I kid you not. When I realised the timing, that number 9 felt strange; it seemed that it *had* to be significant, but I had no idea how it could possibly be of any importance. Niggling at me though it was, I put it down to a passing fancy and tried to push it away, ignore it.

It wouldn't bugger off though, and so, I looked into the meanings and associations of *9*.

It was immediately clear why it had been bugging me, and I was blown away to find that 9 is often associated with "spiritual enlightenment" and "spiritual awakening."

Isn't it strange how these things just appear and come together?

A year later came that conversation, which became a pivotal point in my life; one of those all-important defining moments.

It explained *why* the only spiritual peace I ever feel is in the sea (and to a slightly lesser degree, near the sea), and why I am so physically comfortable near and in the sea. The sea is where I belong, the sea is my *home*.

I finally realised who and what I am: I had an identity.

The sea is part of me, and I am part of the sea; we are one. The sea completes me and makes me whole.

Sedna is my spiritual twin, my sister, an integral part of me. We are one, and together we are whole.

Sedna is that *thing*, unknown and indefinable for so long, for which I had always been searching.

I have found her, and in doing so, I have found myself.

FINDING THE MISSING PIECES WITHIN MY SPIRITUAL TWIN

Sedna didn't automatically appear in my head; after all, I had and still have very little knowledge of these things.

All I knew at the time was that there was another part of me, a spiritual twin, that I had to find. I was very aware of a hole in me, a gap, an emptiness.

Reading and research showed me that there are an awful lot of sea goddesses, and with no idea of who I was looking for I simply started at the beginning.

I thought that I had found the being I was looking for when I came across Amphitrite, but upon learning that she was Poseidon's wife I knew that my search needed to continue. There was no way that someone like *me*, a *nothing*, could be aligned with a deity of such magnitude, such *importance*. To see my inner self in such an esteemed position was laughable: that kind of stature was clearly not for the likes of me. It would not only have been farcical, it would have dishonoured both Amphitrite and Poseidon were I to have placed myself within royalty.

When my reading took me to Sedna I knew immediately, and with utter conviction, that I had found the One.

The similarities between us, in our lives and experiences, are overwhelming. It simply had to be more than mere coincidence.

Finding Sedna has changed me and changed my life.

I now have a vastly enhanced clarity regarding my surroundings. I no longer have to be *in* the sea in order to attain peace; although the feelings of peace and well-being are always strongest there. Just *looking* at the sea, *smelling* the sea, *hearing* the sea, always brings me tranquillity to counter the turmoil in my heart and soul. And of course, I have Sedna to talk to; she's always with me and always there for me.

Yes, I still struggle with my past which means that I still struggle with my present; it's not that all of my hurt and pain have vanished.

However, Sedna has begun to heal at least some of my raw wounds.

I no longer feel alone, no longer cast adrift scared and loveless.

Among all of the difficulties which remain, I *do* now have a *clear and positive sense of self*, even though that positive sense falters and is far from easy to maintain.

I have *belief*, which I lacked before: not only belief in spirituality, but belief in the power and strength of spiritual deities.

Did Sedna draw me to her, or did I draw her to me? This sounds, on the face of it, like the age-old chicken and egg question.

What I *feel*, what I *believe*, is that she and I were *always* kin; I just didn't know it.

That voice, calling me back after so long away, wasn't the sea but was Sedna herself.

I have previously written that I am part of the sea and the sea is part of me; more fundamentally, I am part of Sedna and she is part of me. She is not *outside* me, she is my *inner core*; no less than is water itself at the core of all human bodies.

Sedna and I share something else too: neither of us, I believe, are entirely deserving of our "reputations."

Sedna is considered a "dark" deity, a "vengeful" goddess, I am considered by some (too many for comfort, to be honest) to be "difficult," "hostile," "manipulative." Yet we are all products of our circumstances and experiences. There exists no entity, either spiritual or corporeal, who is wholly "good" or wholly "bad." All of us are a mixture of good, bad, light, dark.
Such is nature.

Sedna's depiction as a "vengeful" goddess came about because, in one of her legends, she required "placating" and "prayers" before she would release the sea-hunters' prey.

Labelling her that way just feels so wrong to me, so *unfair*. Considering all that she suffered is it really so unreasonable for her to want a little placating from time to time? I think not. "Placate" is a synonym for "soothe," "comfort," and "console;" does she not *deserve* some of those things? I think she absolutely does.

Anyone, having been through such abandonment, mutilation, and lack of love would surely wish to be soothed and comforted.

Is it not *harsh* to further degrade her for wanting a taste of these things that she didn't get in life? Is it not adding insult to injury? Is it not rubbing salt into her many wounds?

It is hardly unusual for us to seek comfort from others when we have been hurt; why should it be any different for Sedna?

I wish I were able to give her that comfort: I would hold her tight, stroke and kiss her injured hands, stroke her beautiful face and brush her hair out. I would sing her to sleep, wrapped in my arms.

We all need a little love in our lives and sometimes we need a little comfort, understanding, and empathy. Sedna fills me to the brim with these things, and I ache to give them to her.

TRANSFORMATION

Does my new-found spirituality make any difference in terms of me and the wider population? Am I *better* than anyone else? *Worse*? Am I somehow *more*? Or am I *less*? Am I outside of "the norm"?

I think I'll start with that last question.

"The norm" is whatever society deems it to be, and as such I never *was* the norm.

A girl with no hair is not the norm. A girl brought up to believe that a lack of hair defines her gender as "neither fish nor fowl" is not the norm. A mother terrified of her son is not the norm.

Does having Sedna in my life, my heart, my soul, make me dissimilar, in any *real* way to any other person?

My answer to that is an emphatic "No."

We are all just people, living our lives. We all have hopes, fears, feelings and experiences.

I previously wrote that prior to finding Sedna I'd had no belief; that wasn't quite the truth, now that I think about it. I had long and long believed in animal rights, in equality, in honesty, in integrity, in the necessity for more money to be spent on mental health care...And, it has to be said,

I had far too many beliefs about myself that were negative in the extreme.

My feeling is that Sedna's presence in my life makes a difference only in *my life*; it doesn't alter my status in comparison to other people. I'm not *better* or *more* than the person stood next to me at the bus-stop.

I've got things wrong, done bad things, and will no doubt continue to do so. I've also got things right and done good things, and that too will remain the case. It's human nature that these things happen, they happen to *all of us*. People are people are people.

If anything, because of my childhood and what I was taught to believe about myself, I still see myself as *less* than others.

I stayed in relationships that were *bad,* because I believed that anyone was better than no-one and anyway, what right did I have to expect to be treated well?

I had way too much casual sex, even though I despised myself for it because I strongly believed in fidelity and marriage, because I believed (hoped?) that sex meant affection. And I always hoped desperately that one of those one-night stands would find me worthy enough that he would want to see me again.

I was never the *dumper*, I was always the *dumpee*.

I eventually ended up, and spent far too many of my adult years, within the Bondage and Discipline, Sadism and Masochism (BDSM) scene.

As much as I *did* enjoy the physical side of Dominance/submission (D/s), I was beyond submissive: I was slave. D/s wasn't enough for me, I was looking for Master/slave (M/s): I belonged on my knees, licking boots. I couldn't even conceive of taking on the Domme role. I believed that if I was submissive enough *somebody* would find me *good enough*.

It didn't work; I was used, and I was abused. BDSM is ideal for predators, and the scene is full of prey.

It's important to note that I became friends with a goodly number of people who *did* have long-term, successful D/s or M/s relationships, but the relationships that I entered unfailingly involved a man who was simply a *taker* rather than a Master or even a Dom.

I was slave, not just submissive. I wanted (needed?) a Master, an Owner. I registered myself on the slave register, getting myself my slave number. That number remains assigned to me: sometimes signing up for

something is permanent. The slave register no longer exists, but there remains no way of dissociating myself from that number, and I still remember it.

I stayed with one these men for almost 3 years, trying (and always failing) to be *good enough*. It turned out though that even I had my limits, and there came a time when I left him. I took a beating for it, but *I* had left *him*.

My last M/s relationship was after I had moved back here. It was also my last. It went way beyond anything I had ever agreed to, it completely disregarded *consent*. It was not D/s or M/s, it was physical abuse. And it involved a great deal of pain.

He only got to do it the once: this time not only was *I* the one to leave, but I did it *immediately*. And I knew at that point that I would never let *anyone* touch me again.

I have been celibate ever since; I have no desire for a relationship, and I loathe physical contact.

The only changes that Sedna brings are personal and internal. I have that sense of self, of identity, that I mentioned previously.

Yep, my confidence is still low but it's now kerb-level rather than gutter-level. Sedna increases my awareness of mys*elf* and how

I live my life. My appreciation of all that is nature, not just the sea, is becoming profound and constantly in my thoughts.

In some ways it feels like Sedna is offering me the chance to finally out-run myself, to throw all of the past trauma away. A new identity allows me to develop, at last, a feeling of self-worth and coupled with a little more confidence it's kind of like there's a new me fighting to beat the shit out of the old, hurt, ruined creature that I was.

In this respect Sedna is offering me the opportunity for transformation and freedom.

Let's not forget that what Sedna does is *create life...*

NATURAL MAJIC

I don't practise that which most people would call "magick" every day, or indeed on any day. I'm not a "witch," although there was a time when I tried to learn witchcraft. Those formal, structured lessons, covering the means and methods of various aspects of witchcraft just didn't work for me; I found myself unable to do any of the things I was meant to be learning. And when I did the rituals and tried to cast spells at home I felt quite daft, to be honest, and the spells didn't work. It left me believing that witchcraft is something that people either have or they don't, an innate ability not really any different to any other natural talent. This belief has been reinforced by the fact that the people I know and those I've read about who *do* cast spells, mix up potions, and the whole shebang have done so and had the ability for very many years, often since childhood. Don't get me wrong, I'm not saying that they haven't had to work at it, nurture it, develop it, but they always had that spark within them. I don't have that, and never have had. This doesn't mean that I don't necessarily believe that people *can't* learn, but I do believe that there's a huge difference, and that difference to me is intuitive v mechanical.

Take as an example photography, which is one of my abilities: anyone can learn from the instructions how to use a given camera, but there are no instructions on how to have/get/gain the "eye" and that is the most crucial of factors. It's taken years for me to realise that I don't have to do things the way other people do: that I can, in fact, do things my own way. It's actually ok for me to design, as it were, my own majic and do things in ways that suit me, that feel right for me. I'm allowed to make it all personal. Once I'd figured these things out, everything else began to fall into place. I do things that are "majic" for me and Sedna, not for anyone else and it doesn't matter if anyone else agrees with the way I do things, or gets my way of working, because it's not about them. In fact, I very rarely even talk about what I do and the way I do it. It's not that it's any great secret, I just don't feel the need to share it unless someone specifically asks. It's about me and Sedna, and our relationship; it's also very much about the fact that I am entranced by the simple, every-day majic of nature. That, for me, is really where the majic lies, and it's my perpetual amazement at the wonders of nature that underlies all of the other majic and rituals that I perform. It doesn't even sit right using the word "perform" here, because by and large all that I do is simply live each day with an awareness of all the majic taking place around me.

And my "rituals" are equally natural. Swimming in the sea, feeling at peace and at one with the world while talking to Sedna and knowing that she is with me, collecting hag-stones (pebbles with holes all the way through, which are considered lucky') and driftwood, picking up bags of litter from the beach, taking my camera out to walk the Island, lighting candles for Sedna, sitting quietly listening to Om Aim Sarasweti: all these thigs are my "rituals." If I seriously feel a need to cast a spell, I write whatever it is on a pebble and throw it into the sea while talking to Sedna and asking for her assistance. All of these things are *my* majic and they work for *me*; I believe that it's also a way of working that Sedna accepts and appreciates: after all that was done to her, life is too plain and real to need fancy workings. I believe that the straight forwardness of my approach works as well with her as it does with me. After all, I had to find a way of working that suited us both, because it involves us both. I have, in effect, grown a form of majic that I am comfortable and confident with, and that works for me because it has come from me and my goddess.

Yeah, there are times when I ask certain people for advice or guidance as and when I feel it necessary, but I no longer spend my time buying and/or borrowing endless books and ploughing through them, following other people's directions. I'm most definitely not learning formally; it's not an O-level or a degree with requirements that I must meet in order to pass. It's organic, new, and mine.

The inability to do majic that I used to feel always left me feeling like an outsider, that I didn't belong. I felt separated from others and I felt that I was less than them. Granted, part of that goes back to my childhood, but it's fair to say that at least an equal part of it was because I couldn't do witchcraft. It felt like everyone else that I knew, in that part of my life, could do it except me. That's a lonely place to be. Now I am constantly aware of the majic that surrounds me, and I now know that majic isn't only found in witchcraft. Every sunrise, every sunset, every new bud, every tree... these are all moments of pure majic, and they occur without needing any gowns, incantations, or potions. The only thing that they need is to be noticed. I have a grandson who is three: seeing him born, cutting his cord, watching his first step, hearing each new word... all of those things are pure majic.

Watching him explore the world around him, seeing his joy at every new discovery... pure majic.

Let's return to photography: although I use a digital camera for colour gallery prints, my primary love is b&w film photography. This old photography is nothing less than a blend of alchemy, ritual, and majic. Having shot your film, you need to process (transform) it into negatives. This requires mixing chemicals and ensuring that the mixture is at the right ratio and temperature (alchemy). There are then a number of steps that must be followed to achieve a correctly developed set of negatives (ritual). From the point where you take the film out of the camera to the point where you remove it from the developing tank, you have no idea whatsoever what will actually be on the film. However, with the film transformed into negs and hanging to dry you get your first look at the images you have captured (or indeed, you discover that you used the wrong settings during shooting or you over/under processed the film and all you have got is an un-usable film. And remember that "eye" I mentioned earlier: it has captured what it saw and transferred it via the camera to the film. Majic. When the negs are dry, they are ready for printing: mix up the correct amount of chemicals (alchemy), follow the process (ritual) which enables your enlarger to print your image onto the paper. But the paper is still blank until you continue the ritual by placing the sheet into the developer; then slowly and gradually, the image appears through the fluid onto the paper. Majic. Development is stopped, the image is fixed, washed, and hung to dry; the ritual is complete, and transformation is achieved.

Writing is also an act of majic: transferring whatever is in your mind to paper, transforming thoughts and feelings into words, and in doing so, drawing other people into your world.

The world is full of majic every single day, and it saddens me that so much of it is completely un-noticed. All of that natural majic is for sure important and special because nature's majic has always been there and always will be there. Why is it that my grandson explores absolutely everything and delights in every new discovery? Why does he say "Hello" to the birds and trees, and try to kiss ants? It's because for him, and for all small children, everything is majical; perhaps we would all live happier if we remembered to look and see as children do. Just for a moment each day, discard your adult, experienced, jaded eyes and replace them with the eyes of a toddler; then you will once again see all that real majic. All creatures are welcome in my home: wasps, bees, flies, spiders, frogs, chiggy-wigs (woodlice)...

I also think it's right and fitting to mention those things that we call "luck," "fortune," or "coincidence," and all those times we find ourselves saying "That was a bit odd/strange/spooky." Are these events and occurrences not examples of majic happening to us, being directed at us, by some *other* – nature? Way back, in the late 1980s, I watched a documentary about a Russian singer/songwriter who had come to England in search of more artistic freedom. His songs picked me up and carried me away with an awesome combination of his music and lyrics, which were really the most beautifully expressive poetry. It was an intriguing blend, unlike anything I'd ever heard before. In those days, WH Smith in my nearest town still sold records, and while flicking through them a month or so later, I came across the LP he had recorded during his time in England. It very quickly became one of my all-time favourite albums and was forever on the turntable. When records were replaced by cds, I bought it in the new format, along with some of his other albums. Many years later, in my 30s, on the wonder that is You Tube, I found a video of him performing Om Aim Sarasweti in concert at The Albert Hall; it made me tingle all over with a very strong physical sensation, yet at the same time it filled me with peace. It touched me profoundly and although I recognised that it was a chant, I thought no more of it, even though I watched that film clip repeatedly over the years . Now in 2019, so long after the initial event, I have discovered that Sarasweti is another water goddess; she's a river goddess rather than a sea goddess, but it's still water. She was the wife of Vishnu, then of Brahma, and most surprising of all, she too was mutilated, having her nose cut off by Shiva when he lost his temper after being excluded by Daksha from a sacrifice. I now feel that I have two goddesses within me, working with me. How very lucky am I?

Majic comes in many forms and in many ways; it is not solely the province of those who call themselves "magicians," "magickians," or "majicians."

I don't have an altar, a wand, or any particularly sacred objects. My home is filled with driftwood, pebbles, sea-glass, and shells. I have a glass lighthouse tea-light holder, which I use to shine a light for Sedna. I have photographs of my beautiful coast and sea on my walls. I create mini stone stax using lucky pebbles. I wear only green and/or blue clothes and jewellery, the colours of the sea. The executor of my will is aware that after my death I wish to join Sedna in the sea and the necessary arrangements are in place. It is through all of these things that I honour Sedna; both my entire living space and myself are dedicated to her (and to a lesser extent, Sarasweti)

BEING HUMAN

Negative, "dark," emotions and feelings are a part of every-day living, and everyone has them. If there were no emotions labelled "negative," how could those that are called "positive" exist? We can't have the one without the other, but unfortunately the "negatives" are pointed out, noticed, and commented upon far more than their opposites.

Society has decreed that certain human attributes are "bad": jealousy, anger, frustration, etc; we all feel/experience them at times, but does that make us "bad" people? I think not; they are an emotional response to a situation or circumstances: cause and effect. These are logical and understandable responses, so how can they be "bad" or "wrong"?

I've always believed that it's wrong that Sedna is considered a "dark" goddess because of her anger and desire for placation. Considering what she went through and all that she suffered, is her anger not understandable and justified? Is it not fair that she should wish to be placated? "Placated," after all, means soothed and calmed. Classifying her as "dark" is blaming her for her feelings: a nice bit of victim-blaming.

Our feelings are ours, caused by whatever events occur, and nobody has the right to tell us that they are "bad" or "wrong." This is not Brave New World, where everyone is always happy and content; we live in a world where situations that are hard to handle occur, and these cause those emotions that are undesirable to society. Granted, at these times, we may well not be showing ourselves at our best, but does it make us "bad" people? It makes us *human*: to have no feelings is to be soul-less.

Society often prefers to dismiss and re-label emotions/feelings that it finds difficult to deal with: frustration and/or distress may well be interpreted as anger. Some people, especially those who are paid to work with those who are having emotional difficulties find frustration and distress too much trouble to deal with and it's far easier to label the person as "angry," "obstructive," or "hostile." People are placed under psychiatric "care" because society deems their emotions/feelings/reactions to be unacceptable, wrong, and needing correction. Psychiatry then labels those people as having "personality disorders" or "schizophrenia" and the societal stigma levelled at those people for receiving "care" and because of their diagnosis is such that it causes yet more of the "bad" actions/reactions. This becomes circular and extremely hard to break free from.

There is "good" and "bad," "light" and "dark" in all of us, as there is night and day, sun and moon, dawn and sunset. All these things are part of life and will ever be so.

SIMPLE

I simply talk to Sedna, and to Sarasweti now that I know her, the same as I talk to anyone else. Sometimes, that's no more than a "Hello," "Goodnight," or "I'm thinking of you." Sometimes the speech is in my mind, but more often than not it's spoken out loud and conversational. The brief greetings and acknowledgements are daily occurrences, along with the nightly lighting of the tea-light in the lighthouse.

I talk to both of them most when I'm on the beach or in the sea, or when I'm particularly troubled by something. The beach and the sea: those are places where they are, so that's where my deepest, most meaningful conversations take place.

I've never thought of it as a "communion," it's just me talking to my sisters. I tell them how much I love them and that there will come a time when I will be with them. I tell them, with no small amount of guilt and shame, that I have nothing to give them, no gifts, that all I have to give is myself and I give that willingly and eagerly. I tell them that at that time, when we are together, I will give them all the love and acceptance that they were denied by others. I hope that in this that I too will finally find peace and no longer be judged as lacking.

I ask for their guidance and/or assistance at times of need, and I apologise for having no gifts for them except for myself.

When I am in the sea, I feel that I am being rocked in Sedna's arms; I feel safe, loved, and at peace. I sit on the beach, watching the sun glancing off the ripples, knowing that Sedna is there. I kiss pebbles, ok, I'll tell the truth: I lick pebbles. It's as if, with the salt and sea-water from the pebbles, I am bringing the essence of Sedna right into my centre. When I am in the sea, I can literally feel my pores opening up and absorbing the sea water. I love wearing it, feeling that I am clothed in the sea; I hate having to wash it off.

I was on my way home the other evening; it was the 27th August and I'd been with my grandson and his parents for his third birthday. The first half of the day had been wonderful, but in the afternoon it degenerated into a hellish birthday for a little boy. It left me troubled, distressed, and deeply sad. So, there I was, at about 10.30pm, on the bus on the way home, feeling a whole lot less than peaceful. It suddenly occurred to me that what with the weather, sea conditions, and a host of broken bones, I hadn't been in the sea once this year. For me, who usually begins getting in the sea as close to the 25th April as sea conditions allow, it was utterly appalling to find myself, at what could fairly be called the end of summer, not having been in the sea at all. As soon as I remembered that I hadn't been in the sea, I realised how very badly I needed to be in the sea. I arrived home at about 10.40pm, dropped my bag, grabbed my keys, a towel, and a dry-bag, and headed off for the five-minute walk down to the beach. I didn't take the longest route, but neither did I take the shortest route; I wanted to have a little bit of time to savour what was to come. The beach was empty of people and silent except for the sloshing of gentle waves, everything was a deep, rich, empty black. In the safety and security of solitude, I took off all my clothes, including my headscarf, except my knickers and went for a swim and a chat with Sedna. When I came back out of the water, I licked a pebble, dropped my knickers in the dry-bag, dried myself off and added the towel to the bag, got dressed, and headed back up the hill to home. It had been exactly what I needed: I was still pretty upset on my grandson's behalf and I don't know that I'll ever forget the supposedly adult behaviour I witnessed on what should have been such a special, happy day for that little boy, but I most definitely went off to bed a lot calmer and less stressed than I had been.

The reason for starting swimming on the 25th April each year, by the way, is because that's the date in 2009 when I travelled from my then-home in Bristol back to the Island to sign the lease on the flat where I have lived since I moved in during May 2009. After signing the lease, those years ago, which meant that coming back to my beloved Island was actually going to happen, I went down to the beach and consummated it with a swim. I also promised at that time to take care of the beach and thanked the Island for having me back after I had abandoned her for so long.

Back last spring, I decided that I wanted to have the sea indoors at home, not just the various items that I pick up from the beach. To that end, I bought a small-ish fish-tank and made several trips to the beach with empty, clean bottles to collect enough sea-water to put in it. A visit to the nearest proper aquatic shop taught me that it was rather more involved than putting sea-water in a tank, catching small fish and adding them to the tank. I had to buy a particular sandy/gravel-type stuff for the base of the tank, one chemical to condition the water daily for the first two weeks and another chemical to use ever-after, along with a pump and filter. I learned that the water level would drop due to evaporation, but that

I could not simply top it up with more sea-water, because that would result in over-salinity; I would need to buy special topping-up-marine-tank water. I also learned of the need to occasionally replace a proportion of the current tank water with fresh sea-water. "It's not easy, maintaining a marine tank." I was told. As I already had the sea-water in the tank, adding the gravel mix of course just ended up in a swirling thick cloud, which made the filter work overtime. It didn't seem possible at the time that the water would ever clear, but yeah, it actually did. I added various shells and pebbles from my windowsills and began the chemical routine necessary for fishy inhabitation. Sod's law being what it is, on the day I went to the beach with my net and some tubs, not only didn't I catch anything, I didn't even see anything living except for people. No little crabs in the rock pools or crevices and no little fish. I had to resort to begging a fish from a young lad on holiday; he said he'd used bacon to catch it. A year or so later that fish is still swimming around in my tank, and unimaginative as I am, he's spent that time simply being called "Fishy." It's only when I thought about including all of this about the tank in this book that it occurred to me that the very obvious name is "Sedna." One of the things I really wanted to do this year, as well as swim, was to catch some sea-life to keep my fish company. I'm assuming that company would be welcome, but after a year alone I guess that maybe Sedna likes having the place to herself. When I manage to add some living creature to the tank, the welcome, or lack of, will soon be made obvious I imagine. But anyway, one fish or seven, the fact is that I have achieved my desire to have the outside inside, Chesil Beach in my living room.

Reading through all that I have written for this book, I guess that maybe there is a communion of sorts between Sedna and I; it's just that it's always been too informal for me to give it a title redolent of such scripted ritual, and I really dislike titles. I like to just be and do, no rules and no titles.

Fi Woods LRPS

Fi Woods is a professional photographer and a qualified editor and proofreader. She previously spent many years as a youth worker.

Fi lives on the beautiful Isle of Portland in Dorset and is very much in love with her home and the surrounding sea.

As well as writing, Fi enjoys swimming in the sea, reading, ballet, horse-riding, and spending time with her grandson.

www.ingramcontent.com/pod-product-compliance
Lightning Source LLC
LaVergne TN
LVHW061627070526
838199LV00070B/6608